Unleashing Your Potential: A Journey to Personal Growth

Motivational Hero

CONTENTS

INTRODUCTION

Welcome to "Unleashing Your Potential: A Journey to Personal Growth." In this transformative book, we embark on a quest to unlock the limitless potential within each of us. The path to self-improvement and personal growth is a remarkable journey filled with discovery, challenges, and triumphs. Through these pages, we will explore the essential principles, strategies, and mindsets that can propel you towards becoming the best version of yourself.

In a world brimming with distractions and self-doubt, it is easy to lose sight of our true potential. However, within each of us lies a wellspring of untapped abilities and aspirations waiting to be unleashed. This book is designed to guide you on that journey, providing the tools and insights needed to navigate the obstacles that stand in your way and propel you towards a life of fulfillment and achievement.

1- THE POWER OF BELIEF: UNLOCKING YOUR INNER POTENTIAL

Within every individual resides a well of untapped potential, waiting to be awakened by the power of belief. This chapter explores the transformative impact of belief systems on personal growth and development. By understanding the role belief plays in shaping our actions, we can harness its power to propel us towards our goals and aspirations.

Belief acts as a catalyst, fueling our motivation and determination to overcome obstacles. When we believe in ourselves and our abilities, we unlock the door to possibilities we may have never thought attainable. It is the unwavering belief in our potential that empowers us to take the necessary steps towards personal growth.

Throughout this chapter, we will delve into the psychology of belief and its influence on our thoughts, emotions, and actions. We will explore practical techniques and exercises to strengthen our belief systems and develop unshakeable confidence. By adopting a growth mindset and cultivating positive self-talk, we can rewire our subconscious mind to embrace possibilities and expand our horizons.

Furthermore, we will examine real-life success stories of individuals who have transformed their lives through the power of belief. Their inspiring journeys will serve as beacons of hope, illustrating the incredible heights that can be reached when we tap into our inner reservoirs of potential.

In the subsequent chapters, we will build upon the foundation of belief and delve deeper into various aspects of personal growth. From embracing change and setting goals to cultivating resilience and discovering our passions, each chapter will provide invaluable insights and practical strategies to guide you on your transformative journey.

Prepare yourself for a life-altering experience as we unlock the door to your true potential. Let "Unleashing Your Potential: A Journey to Personal Growth" be your guide as you embark on this transformative quest towards becoming the best version of yourself. Remember, the power to unleash your potential lies within you, waiting to be awakened.

2- EMBRACING CHANGE: OVERCOMING CHALLENGES AND ADVERSITY

Change is an inevitable part of life, and our ability to embrace it is crucial for personal growth and development. In this chapter, we explore the profound impact of embracing change and how it can propel us forward in our journey towards self-improvement.

Change often brings with it uncertainty and discomfort. We may find ourselves hesitant to step out of our comfort zones, clinging to familiarity and resisting the unknown. However, true growth lies beyond the boundaries of familiarity. By embracing change, we open ourselves up to new opportunities, experiences, and perspectives.

One of the key aspects of embracing change is understanding that it is a constant force in our lives. Rather than viewing change as something to be feared or avoided, we can choose to see it as an opportunity for growth and transformation. By cultivating a mindset of adaptability and resilience, we can navigate the ever-changing landscapes of our lives with grace and confidence.

This chapter explores practical strategies for embracing change and overcoming the challenges and adversity that often accompany it. We delve into the importance of self-reflection and self-awareness, as these qualities allow us to understand our reactions to change and uncover the underlying beliefs and fears that may hold us back.

Moreover, we examine the power of mindset in embracing change. By adopting a growth mindset, we can view challenges as opportunities for learning and development. We learn to reframe obstacles as steppingstones towards our goals, and setbacks as valuable lessons that propel us forward.

Throughout this chapter, we will also explore the stories of individuals who have embraced change and triumphed over adversity. Their inspiring journeys serve as testaments to the resilience of the human spirit and provide us with valuable insights and inspiration for our own paths.

In addition to mindset shifts, we will discuss practical strategies for embracing change, such as setting clear goals, developing flexibility, and cultivating a support system. By equipping ourselves with the necessary tools and resources, we can navigate the waves of change with greater ease and confidence.

As you delve into the pages of this chapter, I encourage you to reflect on your own relationship with change. What are the areas in your life where you may be resisting change? How can you cultivate a mindset of openness and adaptability? By embracing change and embracing the unknown, you open yourself up to a world of possibilities and embark on a transformative journey towards personal growth and fulfillment.

Continue the journey of "Unleashing Your Potential: A Journey to Personal Growth" with Chapter 3, where we explore the power of setting goals and creating a roadmap for success.

3- SETTING GOALS: THE PATHWAY TO SUCCESS

Setting goals is like charting a course towards our desired destination. In this chapter, we delve into the power of goal setting and how it serves as a guiding force in our journey towards personal growth and success.

Goals provide us with direction and purpose. They give us something to strive for and help us channel our energy and efforts towards meaningful pursuits. Whether it's achieving a career milestone, improving our health and well-being, or cultivating fulfilling relationships, setting clear and meaningful goals is essential for progress.

The process of setting goals begins with self-reflection. It involves gaining clarity on our values, aspirations, and the vision we hold for our lives. By aligning our goals with our core values, we create a sense of purpose that fuels our motivation and commitment.

In this chapter, we explore various types of goals, such as short-term, long-term, and stretch goals. Short-term goals provide us with immediate targets to work towards, while long-term goals represent our overarching aspirations. Stretch goals push us beyond our comfort zones and encourage us to aim higher, fostering personal growth and self-discovery.

We also delve into the importance of setting SMART goals—goals that are specific, measurable, attainable, relevant, and time-bound. SMART goals provide clarity and structure, making them more actionable and achievable. They enable us to track our progress, celebrate milestones, and make necessary adjustments along the way.

Furthermore, we explore the power of visualization and affirmations in goal setting. By vividly imagining our desired outcomes and consistently reinforcing positive beliefs through affirmations, we create a powerful mindset that supports our journey towards success.

Throughout this chapter, we provide practical strategies and tools to help you set effective goals. From breaking down larger goals into smaller, manageable steps to creating action plans and utilizing visual aids, you will gain insights into the process of goal setting and learn how to implement it in your own life.

We also share stories of individuals who have set and achieved remarkable goals, showcasing the transformative power of focused intention and perseverance. These stories serve as inspiration, reminding us that with dedication and a clear vision, anything is possible.

As you embark on the journey of setting goals, remember to stay flexible and open to adjustments. Life is dynamic, and our goals may evolve as we grow and gain new insights. Embrace the process of goal setting as a continuous cycle of self-improvement and personal growth.

Setting goals is not only about reaching the destination but also about the journey itself. It is about the person you become, the lessons you learn, and the skills you develop along the way. So, embrace the power of goal setting, and let it be your compass as you navigate the path towards success and fulfillment.

Continue your transformative journey with Chapter 4, where we explore the importance of cultivating a positive mindset for growth and resilience.

4- CULTIVATING A POSITIVE MINDSET: SHIFTING PERSPECTIVES FOR GROWTH

Our mindset has a profound impact on how we perceive the world and navigate the challenges that come our way. In this chapter, we explore the transformative power of cultivating a positive mindset and how it serves as a catalyst for personal growth and resilience.

A positive mindset is not about denying the existence of challenges or suppressing negative emotions. Instead, it is about adopting a perspective that allows us to see opportunities within obstacles, cultivate gratitude amidst difficulties, and maintain an optimistic outlook even in the face of adversity.

One of the fundamental aspects of cultivating a positive mindset is self-awareness. By observing our thoughts and emotions, we can identify negative patterns and limiting beliefs that hinder our growth. Awareness empowers us to challenge and reframe negative thinking, replacing it with empowering and constructive thoughts.

In this chapter, we delve into the power of reframing, which involves consciously shifting our perspective to view situations in a more positive light. By reframing challenges as opportunities for learning and growth, we develop resilience and open ourselves up to new possibilities.

We also explore the role of gratitude in cultivating a positive mindset. Gratitude is a transformative practice that shifts our focus from what is lacking to what is abundant in our lives. By regularly expressing gratitude for even the smallest blessings, we cultivate a mindset of appreciation and attract more positivity into our lives.

Moreover, we delve into the impact of self-talk on our mindset. Our internal dialogue shapes our beliefs and influences our actions. By cultivating positive self-talk, we can rewire our minds to focus on our strengths, embrace self-compassion, and foster a sense of self-belief that propels us towards our goals.

Throughout this chapter, we provide practical exercises and strategies to help you cultivate a positive mindset. From practicing mindfulness and meditation to engaging in positive affirmations and surrounding yourself with uplifting influences, you will gain valuable tools to transform your mindset and enhance your personal growth journey.

In addition, we share stories of individuals who have overcome tremendous challenges through the power of a positive mindset. Their stories serve as a testament to the resilience of the human spirit and offer inspiration for embracing positivity in the face of adversity.

Remember, cultivating a positive mindset is an ongoing practice. It requires consistent effort, self-reflection, and a commitment to growth. As you incorporate these principles into your life, you will witness the profound impact they have on your overall well-being and success.

Embrace the power of a positive mindset, and let it guide you on your journey of personal growth and resilience. As you navigate the challenges that come your way, remember that your mindset can be the key that unlocks a world of possibilities.

5- BUILDING RESILIENCE: BOUNCING BACK FROM SETBACKS

Resilience is the inner strength that enables us to bounce back from setbacks, adapt to adversity, and thrive in the face of challenges. In this chapter, we explore the importance of building resilience and how it plays a vital role in our personal growth journey.

Life is filled with ups and downs, and setbacks are an inevitable part of our human experience. However, it is our response to these setbacks that defines our ability to persevere and move forward. Resilience equips us with the tools and mindset necessary to overcome obstacles, learn from failures, and emerge stronger on the other side.

Building resilience starts with developing a growth mindset—a belief that challenges are opportunities for growth and that our abilities can be developed through effort and perseverance. With a growth mindset, setbacks are seen as temporary setbacks, rather than permanent failures.

In this chapter, we delve into the core components of resilience and provide strategies for strengthening each aspect. We explore the importance of self-care, emphasizing the need to prioritize our physical, mental, and emotional well-being. By taking care of ourselves, we build the foundation of resilience, allowing us to better navigate the challenges that come our way.

We also discussed the power of perspective and reframing in building resilience. By shifting our focus from problems to possibilities, we can find meaning and lessons within adversity. This shift in perspective empowers us to approach challenges with optimism and creativity.

Furthermore, we explore the role of support systems in fostering resilience. Cultivating strong relationships and seeking support from others during difficult times provides us with a sense of belonging and encourages us to lean on our support networks when we need it most.

Throughout this chapter, we share stories of individuals who have demonstrated remarkable resilience in the face of adversity. Their stories serve as inspiration, reminding us that resilience is not just about bouncing back—it's about bouncing forward, using setbacks as springboards for growth and transformation.

In addition to practical strategies, we provide exercises and techniques for building resilience. From practicing gratitude and cultivating a growth mindset to developing problem-solving skills and practicing self-compassion, these tools will empower you to navigate challenges with resilience and grace.

Remember, building resilience is a lifelong journey. It is not about avoiding or denying difficulties but rather developing the inner strength and adaptive capacity to face them head-on. By building resilience, you become better equipped to embrace change, overcome obstacles, and continue your personal growth journey with courage and determination.

As you immerse yourself in this chapter, reflect on the challenges you have faced and the lessons you have learned. Embrace the opportunity to cultivate resilience, knowing that each setback is an invitation to grow stronger and wiser.

Continue your transformative journey with Chapter 6, where we explore the process of self-discovery and uncovering your passions and talents.

6- SELF-DISCOVERY: EXPLORING YOUR PASSIONS AND TALENTS

Self-discovery is a transformative journey that allows us to uncover our passions, talents, and authentic selves. In this chapter, we explore the process of self-discovery and how it paves the way for personal growth, fulfillment, and living a purpose-driven life.

At the core of self-discovery is the exploration of who we truly are—our values, interests, strengths, and aspirations. It is a journey of introspection, reflection, and self-awareness that enables us to align our lives with our deepest desires and unlock our true potential.

To embark on the path of self-discovery, we must create the space for introspection. This may involve setting aside time for solitude, journaling, practicing mindfulness, or engaging in activities that nurture self-reflection. By quieting the external noise, we can tune in to our inner voice and gain clarity about our passions and purpose.

In this chapter, we delve into the importance of exploring our passions and interests. When we engage in activities that ignite our enthusiasm and bring us joy, we tap into our natural talents and abilities. Exploring our passions allows us to align our work, hobbies, and relationships with what truly lights us up, leading to a more fulfilling and meaningful life.

We also delve into the discovery of our strengths and unique talents. By recognizing our innate abilities and developing them further, we can leverage our strengths to excel in our pursuits and make a positive impact in the world. Understanding our strengths not only boosts our confidence but also guides us towards paths that align with our natural inclinations.

Furthermore, self-discovery involves gaining clarity about our values—the guiding principles that shape our decisions and actions. When we align our lives with our core values, we experience a sense of authenticity and integrity. Our values become the compass that directs our choices and guides us towards a life that feels true to who we are.

Throughout this chapter, we provide practical exercises and techniques to support your journey of self-discovery. From conducting personal assessments and exploring new interests to seeking feedback and experimenting with different experiences, these tools will help you uncover hidden passions and talents.

Additionally, we share stories of individuals who have embarked on profound journeys of self-discovery, unveiling their true passions and talents. Their stories serve as inspiration, reminding us that the path of self-discovery is unique to each individual and unfolds at its own pace.

As you immerse yourself in this chapter, give yourself permission to explore, experiment, and embrace curiosity. Trust that within you lies a world of untapped potential waiting to be discovered. Embrace the joy and fulfillment that come from aligning your life with your passions and talents.

Continue your transformative journey with Chapter 7, where we delve into the power of taking action and turning your dreams into reality.

7- TAKING ACTION: TURNING DREAMS INTO REALITY

Dreams have the power to inspire, but it is through action that they become reality. In this chapter, we explore the transformative process of taking action and how it propels us towards the fulfillment of our dreams and goals.

While dreams may ignite our imagination and fuel our aspirations, they remain mere fantasies until we take the first step towards turning them into reality. Taking action involves moving beyond the realm of thoughts and ideas and actively pursuing the path that leads to the manifestation of our dreams.

One of the first steps in taking action is setting clear and specific goals. By breaking down our dreams into actionable steps, we create a roadmap that guides our actions and ensures progress. Each goal serves as a milestone that brings us closer to the realization of our dreams.

In this chapter, we explore the importance of planning and strategizing in the pursuit of our dreams. Developing an action plan allows us to organize our efforts, allocate resources effectively, and anticipate potential obstacles. By outlining the necessary steps and deadlines, we increase our chances of success and maintain momentum.

Moreover, we delve into the role of perseverance and commitment in taking action. Along the journey towards our dreams, we may encounter setbacks, obstacles, and moments of self-doubt. However, it is our unwavering determination and resilience that enables us to persevere and keep moving forward.

Throughout this chapter, we provide practical strategies and techniques to support your journey of taking action. From time management and prioritization to cultivating discipline and accountability, these tools empower you to overcome inertia and make consistent progress towards your dreams.

We also explore the concept of mindset in the process of taking action. By cultivating a growth mindset, we view challenges as opportunities for learning and growth. We embrace a belief in our ability to acquire new skills, adapt to changing circumstances, and overcome obstacles. With a growth mindset, we approach challenges with a sense of curiosity and a willingness to learn from both successes and failures.

Additionally, we share stories of individuals who have taken bold actions and turned their dreams into reality. Their stories serve as inspiration, reminding us that it is through determination, perseverance, and consistent action that dreams are brought to life.

As you delve into this chapter, reflect on your own dreams and aspirations. What actions can you take today to move closer to their realization? Embrace the power of action and trust in your ability to create the life you envision.

Continue your transformative journey with Chapter 8, where we explore the importance of self-care and nurturing your mind, body, and soul for holistic   well-being.

8- THE IMPORTANCE OF SELF-CARE: NURTURING YOUR MIND, BODY, AND SOUL

In the pursuit of our dreams and personal growth, it is vital to prioritize self-care. Chapter 8 explores the profound importance of self-care and how nurturing our mind, body, and soul contributes to our overall well-being and success.

Self-care is a holistic practice that involves tending to our physical, mental, and emotional needs. It is about recognizing that our well-being is the foundation upon which we build a fulfilling and purposeful life. When we prioritize self-care, we replenish our energy, cultivate resilience, and enhance our capacity to navigate challenges.

Nurturing our mind begins with cultivating mental wellness. This involves engaging in activities that stimulate our intellect, expand our knowledge, and foster creativity. Reading, learning, pursuing hobbies, and engaging in stimulating conversations are some ways to nurture our minds and promote cognitive growth.

Taking care of our bodies is equally crucial. Physical well-being forms the foundation for overall health and vitality. Regular exercise, nourishing our bodies with wholesome food, and getting adequate rest and sleep are fundamental aspects of self-care. By prioritizing physical health, we enhance our energy levels, boost our immune system, and improve our overall quality of life.

Equally important is tending to our emotional well-being. This involves acknowledging and validating our emotions, practicing self-compassion, and cultivating healthy coping mechanisms. Activities such as journaling, meditation, spending time in nature, and connecting with loved one's help nourish our emotional selves and promote inner harmony.

In this chapter, we delve into practical self-care strategies and rituals that can be incorporated into daily life. We explore the power of mindfulness, stress management techniques, and the importance of establishing healthy boundaries. By carving out dedicated time for self-care, we create space for rejuvenation, self-reflection, and nurturing our inner selves.

Furthermore, we discuss the significance of self-care in preventing burnout and maintaining work-life balance. In a world that often glorifies busyness and productivity, it is essential to prioritize self-care to prevent exhaustion and maintain our well-being. By creating sustainable habits and setting realistic expectations, we can achieve a harmonious integration of work, personal life, and self-care.

Throughout this chapter, we share stories of individuals who have recognized the transformative power of self-care in their lives. Their experiences serve as inspiration, illustrating the profound impact that self-care practices can have on overall well-being and success.

As you immerse yourself in this chapter, reflect on your own self-care practices and consider areas where you can enhance your well-being. Embrace self-care as an essential part of your personal growth journey, knowing that by nurturing your mind, body, and soul, you create the foundation for a flourishing and fulfilling life.

Continue your transformative journey with Chapter 9, where we explore the development of healthy habits as a cornerstone for success and personal growth.

9- DEVELOPING HEALTHY HABITS: CREATING A FOUNDATION FOR SUCCESS

Healthy habits form the building blocks of a successful and fulfilling life. In Chapter 9, we explore the significance of developing healthy habits and how they contribute to personal growth, well-being, and overall success.

Habits shape our daily routines and ultimately determine the direction of our lives. By intentionally cultivating healthy habits, we create a solid foundation that supports our physical, mental, and emotional well-being. These habits empower us to make positive choices, enhance productivity, and lead a balanced and purposeful life.

One of the key aspects of developing healthy habits is self-discipline. It is the ability to consistently choose actions that align with our values and long-term goals, even in the face of temptations or challenges. Through self-discipline, we establish routines that foster positive behaviors and reinforce our commitment to personal growth.

In this chapter, we explore various areas of life where healthy habits can be cultivated. From physical fitness and nutrition to time management and goal setting, we delve into practical strategies and techniques that support the development of healthy habits.

Taking care of our physical health is paramount. Regular exercise, proper nutrition, and adequate sleep are foundational habits that boost our energy, enhance our well-being, and improve our overall quality of life. We explore ways to incorporate physical activity into our daily routines, make conscious food choices, and establish restful sleep patterns.

Mental and emotional well-being are equally important when developing healthy habits. We delve into practices such as mindfulness, gratitude, and self-reflection that promote mental clarity, emotional resilience, and inner peace. Cultivating healthy habits in these areas enables us to manage stress, enhance focus, and maintain a positive mindset.

Another vital aspect of healthy habits is time management. Efficiently allocating our time and setting priorities allows us to make the most of each day and avoid procrastination. We discuss techniques for effective time management, such as goal-oriented planning, setting boundaries, and eliminating distractions, enabling us to maximize productivity and create space for personal growth activities.

Throughout this chapter, we share inspiring stories of individuals who have embraced healthy habits and witnessed transformative changes in their lives. Their experiences serve as a reminder that small, consistent actions can lead to significant outcomes and that developing healthy habits is a lifelong journey.

As you immerse yourself in this chapter, reflect on your current habits and consider areas where positive changes can be made. Embrace the power of healthy habits as catalysts for personal growth, success, and overall well-being. Remember that each small step towards developing healthy habits brings you closer to the life you aspire to live.

Continue your transformative journey with Chapter 10, where we explore the importance of cultivating relationships and building a supportive network for personal growth and fulfillment.

10- CULTIVATING RELATIONSHIPS: BUILDING A SUPPORTIVE NETWORK

Relationships are the fabric of our lives, and cultivating meaningful connections is essential for personal growth and fulfillment. In Chapter 10, we explore the importance of building and nurturing relationships, and how they contribute to our overall well-being and success.

Human beings are social creatures, and we thrive in the presence of positive and supportive relationships. Cultivating relationships involves fostering connections with family, friends, colleagues, mentors, and like-minded individuals who uplift and inspire us on our personal growth journey.

One of the key benefits of cultivating relationships is the support and encouragement we receive from our network. Having a supportive community provides a sense of belonging and offers a safe space for us to express ourselves, seek guidance, and share our triumphs and challenges. These connections act as a source of motivation, accountability, and inspiration, propelling us forward in our pursuit of personal growth.

In this chapter, we delve into the qualities and dynamics of healthy relationships. We explore the importance of open communication, trust, empathy, and mutual respect. By fostering these qualities, we create a solid foundation for authentic connections that promote personal growth and well-being.

Furthermore, we discuss the concept of reciprocal relationships—those based on mutual support and shared goals. These relationships involve a give-and-take dynamic, where both parties contribute to each other's growth and success. By surrounding ourselves with individuals who uplift and challenge us, we create an environment that nurtures personal development.

We also explore the significance of mentorship and learning from others. Mentors provide guidance, wisdom, and invaluable insights based on their experiences. By seeking mentorship, we gain access to a wealth of knowledge and support, accelerating our personal growth journey.

Throughout this chapter, we provide practical strategies for cultivating and nurturing relationships. From active listening and practicing empathy to engaging in meaningful conversations and offering support, these techniques help strengthen our connections and foster a supportive network.

In addition, we share inspiring stories of individuals who have experienced the transformative power of relationships. Their stories illustrate the profound impact that positive connections can have on personal growth, resilience, and overall well-being.

As you immerse yourself in this chapter, reflect on your current relationships and consider areas where you can invest more time and effort. Nurture the connections that uplift and inspire you and seek opportunities to build new relationships that align with your personal growth goals.

Remember, the quality of our relationships profoundly impacts our happiness, success, and personal growth. Embrace the power of cultivating relationships and building a supportive network as you continue your transformative journey towards a more fulfilling and purposeful life.

Continue your exploration of personal growth with Chapter 11, where we delve into the process of overcoming fear and stepping outside your comfort zone.

11- OVERCOMING FEAR: STEPPING OUTSIDE YOUR COMFORT ZONE

Fear can be a powerful force that holds us back from reaching our full potential. In Chapter 11, we explore the transformative process of overcoming fear and stepping outside our comfort zones, as it is through these courageous actions that personal growth and extraordinary achievements become possible.

Our comfort zone is a psychological state where we feel safe and familiar. It is a place where we experience minimal anxiety or stress. However, true growth and personal development lie beyond the boundaries of our comfort zone. It is in those uncharted territories that we find new opportunities, learn valuable lessons, and unlock our true potential.

In this chapter, we delve into the nature of fear and its impact on personal growth. We examine the various types of fear, such as fear of failure, fear of rejection, and fear of the unknown. By understanding the root causes of our fears, we gain insight into how they hold us back from embracing new experiences and realizing our dreams.

Overcoming fear requires courage and a willingness to face our discomfort head-on. It involves challenging our limiting beliefs and reframing our perspective on failure and rejection. By recognizing that failure is not a reflection of our worth but rather an opportunity for growth, we can reframe fear as a steppingstone towards personal development.

We explore practical strategies for stepping outside our comfort zones and conquering fear. Gradual exposure, setting achievable goals, and seeking support from mentors or accountability partners are some of the approaches we discuss. These strategies help us build resilience, expand our comfort zones, and cultivate a mindset of curiosity and growth.

Moreover, we share inspiring stories of individuals who have overcome their fears and achieved remarkable success. Their experiences serve as reminders that greatness often lies on the other side of fear. By stepping outside their comfort zones, they have unleashed their full potential and created extraordinary lives.

Throughout this chapter, we also emphasize the importance of self-compassion and self-care in the process of overcoming fear. It is crucial to be gentle with ourselves, celebrate small victories, and acknowledge that growth takes time. By nurturing our well-being and practicing self-compassion, we build the resilience necessary to navigate the challenges that arise on our journey of personal growth.

As you delve into this chapter, reflect on the fears that may be holding you back from pursuing your dreams and goals. Embrace the discomfort and recognize that stepping outside your comfort zone is where true growth and transformation occur. With each courageous step, you break free from the constraints of fear and open yourself up to a world of possibilities.

Continue your transformative journey with Chapter 12, where we explore the art of failure and how it can be a valuable teacher on the path to personal growth and success.

12- THE ART OF FAILURE: LEARNING AND GROWING FROM MISTAKES

Failure is often perceived as something negative, but in reality, it is an essential part of the journey towards personal growth and success. In Chapter 12, we delve into the art of failure and how it can serve as a valuable teacher, providing valuable lessons and opportunities for growth.

Failure is not the end of the road; it is a steppingstone on the path to success. When we reframe our perspective and view failure as a natural part of the learning process, we open ourselves up to invaluable insights and transformative experiences. It is through failure that we gain resilience, develop problem-solving skills, and refine our strategies.

In this chapter, we explore the importance of embracing failure and extracting the lessons it offers. By examining our failures with a growth mindset, we can identify areas for improvement, gain new perspectives, and adjust our approach accordingly. Failure becomes a catalyst for innovation and personal development.

We also delve into the concept of embracing failure as an opportunity for self-discovery. In moments of failure, we learn about our strengths, weaknesses, and areas where we can grow. By embracing our failures with self-compassion and curiosity, we uncover hidden potential and develop a deeper understanding of ourselves.

Throughout this chapter, we provide practical strategies for learning and growing from failure. We explore techniques such as reflection, self-assessment, and seeking feedback. By engaging in these practices, we can extract valuable lessons from our failures and apply them to future endeavors.

Moreover, we share stories of individuals who have experienced significant failures but ultimately achieved great success. Their stories serve as inspiration, reminding us that failure is not a permanent state but rather a temporary setback on the path to greatness. By persisting and learning from their failures, these individuals have reached new heights and achieved their goals.

Additionally, we discuss the importance of resilience and self-belief in navigating failure. When we embrace failure as a natural part of the journey, we develop the resilience necessary to bounce back and persevere. Cultivating a belief in our abilities and maintaining a positive mindset enables us to view failures as opportunities for growth rather than setbacks.

As you immerse yourself in this chapter, reflect on your own experiences with failure and consider the lessons you have learned. Embrace failure as a valuable teacher and an essential part of the process of personal growth. Through the art of failure, you will discover resilience, strength, and the courage to continue your transformative journey.

Continue your exploration of personal growth with Chapter 13, where we delve into the importance of finding balance and harmonizing work and life for overall well-being and success.

13- FINDING BALANCE: HARMONIZING WORK AND LIFE FOR WELL-BEING AND SUCCESS

In today's fast-paced world, finding balance between work and personal life has become essential for overall well-being and success. In Chapter 13, we explore the importance of harmonizing work and life, and how it contributes to our happiness, fulfillment, and sustained personal growth.

Achieving a healthy work-life balance involves prioritizing and allocating time and energy to various areas of our lives, including work, family, relationships, hobbies, and self-care. It is about creating a harmonious integration of these aspects, rather than allowing one to dominate at the expense of others.

One of the key benefits of finding balance is enhanced well-being. When we devote time to activities that nourish our mind, body, and soul, we experience greater overall satisfaction and happiness. Balancing work and personal life allow us to recharge, maintain physical and mental health, and cultivate meaningful relationships.

In this chapter, we delve into practical strategies for finding balance. We explore techniques such as effective time management, setting boundaries, and practicing self-care. By prioritizing our tasks, setting realistic goals, and establishing healthy boundaries, we can create space for both work and personal life, reducing stress and promoting well-being.

We also discuss the importance of setting clear priorities and aligning our actions with our values. By understanding our core values and defining what truly matters to us, we can make conscious decisions and allocate time and energy accordingly. This alignment ensures that we invest in activities that align with our goals and bring us joy and fulfillment.

Moreover, we explore the significance of communication and collaboration in achieving work-life balance. By effectively communicating our needs and boundaries with employers, colleagues, and loved ones, we create understanding and support. Collaboration with others helps distribute responsibilities, fostering a sense of shared responsibility and reducing the burden of trying to do everything alone.

Throughout this chapter, we share stories of individuals who have successfully achieved work-life balance and reaped the benefits in their personal and professional lives. Their experiences serve as inspiration, reminding us that it is possible to create a fulfilling and harmonious life by prioritizing balance.

As you immerse yourself in this chapter, reflect on your current work-life balance and identify areas that may require adjustments. Embrace the importance of finding balance and integrate strategies that allow you to nurture all aspects of your life. Remember, achieving work-life balance is a continuous process that requires self-awareness, adaptability, and a commitment to personal well-being and success.

Continue your transformative journey with Chapter 14, where we explore the significance of continuous learning and personal development for staying relevant and thriving in a rapidly changing world.

14- THE POWER OF CONTINUOUS LEARNING: THRIVING IN A RAPIDLY CHANGING WORLD

In a world that is constantly evolving, continuous learning and personal development are crucial for staying relevant and thriving. In Chapter 14, we explore the significance of lifelong learning, the power of personal development, and how they contribute to personal growth, adaptability, and success.

Continuous learning is an ongoing process of acquiring new knowledge, skills, and perspectives throughout our lives. It is the commitment to expand our horizons, challenge our assumptions, and embrace the ever-changing landscape of knowledge and information.

One of the key benefits of continuous learning is personal growth. By engaging in learning activities, we broaden our understanding, gain new insights, and develop critical thinking skills. Continuous learning allows us to adapt to new situations, embrace innovation, and foster a growth mindset that propels us forward.

In this chapter, we explore different avenues for continuous learning. We delve into formal education, such as enrolling in courses, pursuing higher degrees, and attending workshops and seminars. We also explore informal learning, including reading books, listening to podcasts, participating in online communities, and engaging in self-directed learning.

Personal development goes hand in hand with continuous learning. It involves intentional efforts to enhance our personal and professional skills, cultivate self-awareness, and foster a sense of purpose and fulfillment.

Personal development enables us to unlock our potential, overcome limitations, and lead a more meaningful and satisfying life.

Furthermore, we discuss the importance of embracing a growth mindset in the process of continuous learning and personal development. A growth mindset is the belief that our abilities and intelligence can be developed through dedication and effort. By embracing a growth mindset, we view challenges as opportunities for growth, persist in the face of setbacks, and approach learning with enthusiasm and curiosity.

Throughout this chapter, we provide practical strategies for incorporating continuous learning and personal development into our lives. We explore techniques such as goal setting, creating learning plans, seeking mentors, and building a supportive learning network. These strategies empower us to design our own learning journeys and make progress towards our personal and professional goals.

Moreover, we share stories of individuals who have embraced continuous learning and personal development, achieving remarkable success and personal fulfillment. Their experiences serve as inspiration, reminding us of the transformative power of lifelong learning and the limitless possibilities it brings.

As you immerse yourself in this chapter, reflect on your own learning journey and identify areas where you can incorporate continuous learning and personal development. Embrace the power of growth and commit to a lifelong pursuit of knowledge, skills, and self-improvement. Remember, in a rapidly changing world, those who embrace continuous learning are the ones who thrive and make a lasting impact.

Continue your transformative journey with Chapter 15, the final chapter, where we reflect on the significance of gratitude and celebrate the growth and progress made throughout the personal growth journey.

15- GRATITUDE: EMBRACING APPRECIATION AND CELEBRATING GROWTH

In the final chapter of our transformative journey, we explore the profound power of gratitude and its role in personal growth, well-being, and fulfillment. Chapter 15 is a celebration of the growth and progress made throughout our personal growth journey, and a reminder to embrace gratitude as a guiding principle for a fulfilling life.

Gratitude is the practice of acknowledging and appreciating the blessings, experiences, and people that enrich our lives. It is a mindset that shifts our focus from what is lacking to what is abundant, from negativity to positivity, and from self-centeredness to interconnectedness. By cultivating gratitude, we cultivate joy, contentment, and a deeper sense of meaning.

In this chapter, we delve into the transformative effects of gratitude on our well-being. Research has shown that practicing gratitude leads to improved mental health, increased happiness, and enhanced resilience. When we consciously acknowledge the blessings in our lives, we foster a positive outlook, reduce stress, and nurture our relationships.

We explore various ways to incorporate gratitude into our daily lives. From keeping a gratitude journal and expressing appreciation to others to practicing mindfulness and reflecting on moments of gratitude, we discover that gratitude is a practice that can be cultivated and integrated into our routines. By making gratitude a habit, we invite more positivity and abundance into our lives.

Furthermore, we reflect on the growth and progress made throughout our personal growth journey. We celebrate the milestones, the lessons learned, and the challenges overcome. We recognize that personal growth is not always linear, but rather a continuous process of learning, evolving, and embracing new experiences.

We invite self-reflection and encourage the reader to take a moment to appreciate their own personal growth journey. We encourage celebrating the achievements, big and small, and acknowledging the resilience and courage it took to overcome obstacles and embrace personal transformation.

Throughout this chapter, we share stories of individuals who have embraced gratitude as a guiding principle in their lives. Their experiences serve as inspiration, reminding us of the profound impact gratitude can have on our well-being, relationships, and overall fulfillment.

As we conclude this transformative journey, we invite you to continue practicing gratitude and incorporating it into your daily life. Embrace the lessons learned, the growth achieved, and the connections made along the way. By cultivating gratitude, we create a foundation of appreciation that allows us to navigate future challenges with resilience and grace.

Remember, the journey of personal growth is ongoing. Embrace gratitude as a constant companion and a guiding light, illuminating the path ahead. With gratitude in our hearts, we embark on a life of meaning, joy, and continued growth.

May your personal growth journey be filled with gratitude, fulfillment, and limitless possibilities.

www.ingramcontent.com/pod-product-compliance
Lightning Source LLC
Chambersburg PA
CBHW072225290526
45794CB00007B/2897